Target
Get back on track

GRADE 9

Edexcel GCSE (9-1)
English Language
Writing

Julie Hughes

D1350269

Pearson

Published by Pearson Education Limited, 80 Strand, London, WC2R ORL.

www.pearsonschoolsandfecolleges.co.uk

Text © Pearson Education Limited 2017
Produced and typeset by Tech-Set Ltd, Gateshead
Original illustrations © Pearson Education Ltd 2017

The right of Julie Hughes to be identified as author of this work has been asserted by her in accordance with the Copyright, Designs and Patents Act 1988.

First published 2017

20 19 18 17
10 9 8 7 6 5 4 3 2

British Library Cataloguing in Publication Data
A catalogue record for this book is available from

ISBN 978 0435 18330 1

Printed in Slovakia by Neografia

Acknowledgements
The publisher would like to thank the following for their kind permission to reproduce their photographs:

(Key: b-bottom; c-centre; l-left; r-right; t-top)

123RF.com: 1l, 3; **Shutterstock.com**: 24Novembers 6l, 7l, Pedro Monteiro 6r, 7r, steve estvanik 1r, 4

All other images © Pearson Education

This workbook has been developed using the Pearson Progression Map and Scale for English.

To find out more about the Progression Scale for English and to see how it relates to indicative GCSE 9–1 grades go to www.pearsonschools.co.uk/ProgressionServices

Helping you to formulate grade predictions, apply interventions and track progress.

Any reference to indicative grades in the Pearson Target Workbooks and Pearson Progression Services is not to be used as an accurate indicator of how a student will be awarded a grade for their GCSE exams.

You have told us that mapping the Steps from the Pearson Progression Maps to indicative grades will make it simpler for you to accumulate the evidence to formulate your own grade predictions, apply any interventions and track student progress. We're really excited about this work and its potential for helping teachers and students. It is, however, important to understand that this mapping is for guidance only to support teachers' own predictions of progress and is not an accurate predictor of grades.

Our Pearson Progression Scale is criterion referenced. If a student can perform a task or demonstrate a skill, we say they are working at a certain Step according to the criteria. Teachers can mark assessments and issue results with reference to these criteria which do not depend on the wider cohort in any given year. For GCSE exams however, all Awarding Organisations set the grade boundaries with reference to the strength of the cohort in any given year. For more information about how this works please visit: https://qualifications.pearson.com/en/support/support-topics/results-certification/understanding-marks-and-grades.html/Teacher

The activities in this workbook have been developed to support students in attaining the 10th, 11th and 12th Steps in the Progression Scale, focusing on those barriers to progression identified in the Pearson Progression Scale.

10th Step	11th Step	12th Step
Ideas are selected and structured with some consideration of purpose and intention before writing, and some consideration of vocabulary and sentence structure for effect during and after writing. Paragraphs and sentence structures are manipulated for effect, and a broad vocabulary selected for clarity, concision, precision and originality.	Writing design makes a significant contribution to purpose and intention, with frequent consideration of whole text and language choices during and after writing. Paragraph and sentence structures make a significant contribution to pace, tone or register, and a broad, sophisticated vocabulary is carefully selected with consideration of purpose and intention.	Writing is designed to achieve purpose and intention, with significant revisions to whole text, and language choices during and after writing. Paragraph and sentence structures are crafted to control pace, tone and/or register, and a broad and sophisticated vocabulary makes a significant contribution to purpose and intention.

Unit title and skills boost	Pearson Progression Scale: Barriers (difficulties students may encounter when working towards this step)	Assessment Objectives
Unit 1 Generating ideas – imaginative writing **Skills boost 1** How do I come up with an original narrative? **Skills boost 2** How do I decide on a narrative viewpoint? **Skills boost 3** How do I develop my narrative to create impact for the reader?	• May lack confidence in 'breaking rules' e.g. mixing tenses in narrative, using highly figurative language in a non-fiction text; addressing the reader directly. (10th Step) • May not fully understand how to create different narrative voices or perspectives or how to fully adapt style and vocabulary matched to different viewpoints, audiences and purposes. (11th Step) • May not give enough consideration to selecting or shaping ideas for the prescribed audience, reverting instead to selecting ideas to appeal to the actual audience of peers, teacher, examiner etc. (11th Step) • Endings still likely to be least successful feature of texts, especially in timed tasks. (10th Step/11th Step)	Communicate clearly, effectively and imaginatively (AO5)
Unit 2 Generating ideas – transactional writing **Skills boost 1** How do I establish a point of view that suits my purpose? **Skills boost 2** How do I select ideas to suit my audience? **Skills boost 3** How do I generate ideas to build towards a powerful conclusion?		Communicate clearly, effectively and imaginatively (AO5)
Unit 3 Structuring your ideas – imaginative writing **Skills boost 1** How do I shape my narrative for maximum impact? **Skills boost 2** How do I manipulate the structure of my ideas for impact? **Skills boost 3** How do I start and end my narrative for greatest impact?		Organise information and ideas (AO5)
Unit 4 Structuring your ideas – transactional writing **Skills boost 1** How do I shape my ideas? **Skills boost 2** How do I write an effective opening and conclusion? **Skills boost 3** How do I sequence and develop my ideas?		Organise information and ideas (AO5)

Unit 5 Cohesion – making it clear **Skills boost 1** How do I guide the reader through my writing? **Skills boost 2** How do I structure paragraphs to link my ideas? **Skills boost 3** How do I develop my ideas without repeating myself?	• May lack sufficiently wide or sophisticated range of discourse markers e.g. to highlight distinct steps in an argument or maximise use of contrasts or examples. (11th Step)	Communicate clearly, effectively and imaginatively (AO5)
Unit 6 Making your meaning clear – sentences **Skills boost 1** How do I use single-clause sentences to clarify my meaning? **Skills boost 2** How do I experiment with sentence structure to clarify my meaning? **Skills boost 3** How do I use advanced punctuation to clarify my meaning?	• May have a limited range of complex text models e.g. hybrid texts which mix styles, on which to draw in own writing. (10th Step) • May lack the automatic control of sentence types and punctuation that would allow for a range of rhetorical effects, especially when writing in exam conditions. (11th Step)	Use sentence structures for clarity, purpose and effect (AO6)
Unit 7 Writing paragraphs and sentences to create impact **Skills boost 1** How do I structure my paragraphs to engage the reader? **Skills boost 2** How do I experiment with sentence structure to create impact? **Skills boost 3** How do I use advanced punctuation to create impact?	• May be unwilling to take risks e.g. using verbless sentences or very short paragraphs in case results are considered inaccurate. (10th Step) • May miss opportunities to exploit variation in textual rhythms e.g. by contrasting a highly developed longer paragraph with an emphatic single sentence paragraph to create abrupt changes of mood, or by sequencing sentences within a paragraph to withhold information until a final moment of revelation. (12th Step) • May lack awareness of the possibilities of punctuation for effect, considering it a grammatical feature rather than a stylistic choice. (10th Step)	Use a range of vocabulary and sentence structures for clarity, purpose and effect (AO6)
Unit 8 Making your meaning clear – choosing precise vocabulary **Skills boost 1** How do I select vocabulary to create the right tone? **Skills boost 2** How do I use abstract nouns? **Skills boost 3** How do I choose precise vocabulary for clarity and concision?	• May not be able to sustain intended effects across a text e.g. maintaining ironic tone or character's distinctive voice through dialogue. (10th Step) • May use an over-elaborate style e.g. with heavy use of figurative language when a sparer, sparser style might be more appropriate. (12th Step)	Use a range of vocabulary and sentence structures for clarity, purpose and effect (AO6)
Unit 9 Selecting vocabulary for impact and effect **Skills boost 1** How do I explore vocabulary choices and their effects? **Skills boost 2** How do I use figurative language for effect? **Skills boost 3** How do I ensure my vocabulary creates the right effect?	• Use of figurative language may be overdone or lack cohesion e.g. mixing metaphors. (10th Step) • May use an over-elaborate style e.g. with heavy use of figurative language when a sparer, sparser style might be more appropriate. (12th Step) • May not appreciate or have considered the significance of textual rhythm as a factor in effective texts. (10th Step)	Use a range of vocabulary and sentence structures for clarity, purpose and effect (AO6)

Contents

① Generating ideas – imaginative writing

This unit will help you generate ideas for an imaginative writing task. The skills you will build are to:

- take an innovative approach to the task
- develop an original narrative voice
- create impact and meaning for the reader.

In the exam, you will be asked to tackle an imaginative writing task such as the one below. This unit will help you to plan your own response to the question.

> **Exam-style question**
>
> Look at the images provided.
>
> Write about waking up in a strange place.
>
> Your response could be real or imagined. You may wish to base your response on one of the images.
>
>
>
> (40 marks)

The three key questions in the **skills boosts** will help you prepare your response.

> **1** How do I come up with an original narrative?
>
> **2** How do I decide on a narrative viewpoint?
>
> **3** How do I develop my narrative to create impact for the reader?

Look at one student's story plan on the next page. It was written in response to a similar question.

Write about a time when you, or someone you know, took a long journey.

Get up from seat, heart pounding, hands clammy, hall silent

Long walk to front of hall, silence oppressive, begin to reflect on starting piano at age 5

Journey to stage for piano recital

Reach stage, knees buckling, think about what I have missed out on to get here

See parents, stumble slightly, reflect on sacrifices they have made for me

(1) The student has taken an innovative approach to the task. Note down ✐ three techniques the writer has used to engage the reader.

....

....

....

....

....

....

....

....

(2) The plan does not include an ending. Make notes ✐ for an original end to the story.

....

....

....

....

....

....

....

....

(3) The narrator in this story is the person taking the journey. Think of two other narrators who could have told the story.

1 ....

2 ....

How do I come up with an original narrative?

One way to come up with an original narrative is to ignore the most obvious ideas and try to think of a more unusual way to approach the question.

Use the picture stimulus to help you with original ideas. For example:

- look at who or what is in the image
- think about the background of the picture.

(?) What would it be like if I woke up on, or near, a camel?

(?) What would it be like if I were the camel and someone strange woke up on my back?

(?) What if I woke up, looked out of my high-rise building, and could see a camel?

(1) Look at the picture and use the bullet points and the questions around the picture to come up with two original story ideas.

Story idea 1:

Story idea 2:

(2) Choose your best ideas, then note ✎ two narrators for your story and the mood or genre to be created by each narrator.

Narrator 1	Mood/genre created
....	....
....	....

Narrator 2	Mood/genre created
....	....
....	....

2 How do I decide on a narrative viewpoint?

When you have generated some ideas, you can begin to think about narrative viewpoint. This can be used to manipulate readers' feelings.

First-person narration encourages a reader to sympathise with his/her actions and feelings.	Third-person narration allows the writer to manipulate a reader's feelings by passing judgement on the characters' thoughts and actions.	Omniscient third-person narration allows the writer to be all-knowing. This allows the reader to know the thoughts and feelings of all the characters.
Can be used to withhold information from the reader – a narrator may not understand the full story.	Can be used to create dramatic irony – where the reader knows more about the plot than the characters.	
Example: *A tug on my reins made me glance back into the gloom. Jamal was definitely hiding something sinister on my back.*	Example: *Fingers twitching on his whip, ignoring the blood already seeping from its open wounds, Jamal dug his heels deep into the weary camel's flesh.*	Example: *The boy clung on tightly to the saddle as Jamal whipped the poor camel mercilessly. Both had no thought for anything but getting home.*

(1) Which viewpoint above would most suit the narrative about the camel finding someone waking up on its back? Write 🖉 two sentences to explain your choice.

....

....

....

....

(2) What narrative viewpoint would you choose to write a comic story about a penguin waking up on the deck of this ship? Explain 🖉 your choice.

....

....

....

....

....

....

....

(3) Now change the genre by using a different narrative viewpoint. Explain 🖉 your choice.

....

....

....

....

③ How do I develop my narrative to create impact for the reader?

Think about how you want your reader to feel. Do you want to unsettle, scare, amuse, amaze or thrill them, for example?

Look at one student's plan to moralise (tell a story with a moral message).

Exposition: Camel owner crossing desert to sell stolen jewels. Boy wakes up lost in desert and sneaks onto camel's back.	**Conflict:** Camel owner sees boy and thinks he is stealing from bags. Boy clings on.	**Climax:** Camel owner pushes boy off camel. Boy left to die in desert. Camel owner gets to town and is arrested selling stolen jewels.	**Conclusion:** In prison, the camel owner discovers there was a reward for finding the boy, who is the son of a prince.

① Look again at the exam-style question on page 1. Use the table below to develop ✏ two ideas for your narrative. For example, you could choose to unsettle or scare; moralise (for instance, your narrator or main character learns a valuable lesson); amuse, amaze or thrill your readers.

Exposition	Conflict	Climax	Conclusion
First idea:			
Second idea:			

Sample response

To plan an original narrative task, you need to:

- ignore obvious ideas and think of an innovative approach
- think about the effect of narrative viewpoint on genre and mood
- develop ideas so they have a specific impact on a reader.

Look at this exam-style writing task.

Exam-style question

Look at the images provided. Write about being watched.

Your response could be real or imagined.

You may wish to base your response on one of the images.

(40 marks)

Then look at this student's thoughts for an original response to the question.

| (?) Narrator is a teenager; watcher is Dad who cannot let go and let narrator grow up. Describe walk to school knowing Dad is watching. | (?) Narrator is girlfriend of man in picture; watcher can't let go and stalks girlfriend. Girlfriend gets scared. | (?) Man in building stealing from flat, being watched by CCTV camera operator. Camera operator realises it is her flat. | (?) CCTV camera zooms in on footballer sitting in flat alone. He reflects on career being watched by large crowds. |

(1) Choose the idea that you think would create the most innovative story. Which narrative viewpoint would be most effective for the idea you chose? Explain (✏) your choice.

....

....

....

(2) Develop (✏) one of the ideas so that it has specific impact for the reader.

Your turn!

You are now going to plan your response to this exam-style task.

Exam-style question

Look at the images provided. Write about being watched.

Your response could be real or imagined.

You may wish to base your response on one of the images.

(40 marks)

1 Note down ✏ three original story ideas that you might use in response to this task. Aim to sum up each idea in just one sentence.

Story idea 1: ....

....

....

....

Story idea 2: ....

....

....

....

Story idea 3: ....

....

....

....

....

2 Choose your most innovative idea. Decide what narrative viewpoint to take and the impact you want to have on your readers. Write ✏ **two** sentences about the mood or genre your story will create.

....

....

....

....

....

....

....

....

....

3 Now plan ✏ your response to the above exam-style question on paper.

Review your skills

Check up

Review your response to the exam-style question on page 7. Tick ⊘ the column to show how well you think you have done each of the following.

	Not quite ⊘	Nearly there ⊘	Got it! ⊘
generated an original story idea	☐	☐	☐
decided on a narrative viewpoint	☐	☐	☐
developed a story to create impact for the reader	☐	☐	☐

Look over all of your work in this unit.

Note down 🖉 three pieces of advice you would give to a student who wants to generate original ideas for a story.

1. ....
....
....

2. ....
....
....

3. ....
....
....

Need more practice?

Develop an original response to the exam-style question below.

Exam-style question

Write about an experience in which honesty and/or dishonesty played an important role.

Your response could be real or imagined.

(40 marks)

How confident do you feel about each of these **skills?** Colour 🖉 in the bars.

1 How do I come up with an original narrative?

2 How do I decide on a narrative viewpoint?

3 How do I develop my narrative to create impact for the reader?

② Generating ideas – transactional writing

This unit will help you learn how to generate ideas for a transactional writing task. The skills you will build are to:

- identify and establish a point of view
- select key points that are appropriate for the audience
- develop appropriate ideas that support a firm conclusion.

In the exam, you will be asked to tackle writing tasks such as the one below. This unit will prepare you to write your own response to this question.

Exam-style question

Write an article for a national newspaper about the benefits of modern technology for older people.

You could write about:

- what types of technology are available
- how technology will make their lives easier
- where to get help with modern technology

as well as any other ideas you might have.

(40 marks)

The three key questions in the **skills boosts** will help you generate ideas when you are writing to present a viewpoint.

1 How do I establish a point of view that suits my purpose?

2 How do I select ideas to suit my audience?

3 How do I generate ideas to build towards a powerful conclusion?

Look at one student's plan for an answer to a similar question on the next page.

Write a speech for a school assembly, exploring the idea that the internet is a dangerous tool.

1. The internet is 'anonymous'.	No way of knowing if some internet contacts are dangerous. Unscrupulous people can pose as legitimate. Leaves teenagers open to paedophiles and scammers.
2. Abundance of information.	Infinite research possibilities. Can research family tree. Find tips for hobbies. Online news.
3. It encourages body shaming.	FOMO and pressure to have perfect body/life. No way to stop online abuse. Causes serious mental health issues.
4. Unlimited communication.	People all over the world can share ideas. Can find long-lost relatives.

(1) Look at one student's notes above. Which of the following statements best sums up this student's point of view? Tick it/them. ✓

☐ The student feels the internet is a dangerous tool for teenagers.

☐ It is hard to see a definite point of view.

☐ The student feels the internet has both advantages and disadvantages.

☐ The student feels that the internet makes a positive contribution to teenagers' lives.

(2) Read carefully the details in the student's plan.

a Which details do not suit the audience? Underline (A) them. Explain (✐) your choices.

....

....

....

....

....

....

b Which points most powerfully suit the audience and purpose? Circle (A) them. Explain (✐) your choices.

....

....

....

....

....

....

1 How do I establish a point of view that suits my purpose?

To make your writing more powerful it is a good idea to establish a strong overall point of view.

Look again at the exam-style question from page 9.

Exam-style question

Write an article for a national newspaper about the benefits of modern technology for older people.

(1) For the purpose of the article, which comment provides the most powerful overall point of view? Tick one. ✓

	Modern technology brings many benefits to older people.
	Modern technology is a powerful tool in the fight against ageing.
	Keeps them in touch with the modern world and keeps them in tune with young people.
	Modern technology has advantages and disadvantages.

(2) Write ✏ one or two sentences explaining your choice.

....

....

....

....

....

(3) Which point of view is the weakest for the purpose? Write ✏ one or two sentences explaining your choice.

....

....

....

....

....

(4) How do you feel about older people using technology? Write ✏ one more powerful point of view.

....

....

....

....

....

2 How do I select ideas to suit my audience?

When you have established your overall point of view, you need to generate ideas that suit your audience. To do this you need to think carefully about:

- how wide your potential audience is
- the needs, interest and situation of your audience
- your audience's points of view.

Exam style question

Write an article for a national newspaper about the benefits of modern technology for older people.

(1) Make notes 🖉 with ideas about the needs, interests and situation of different possible audiences: senior citizens, middle-aged adults, young adults, and teenagers, for the above article.

Senior citizens – might be short of money	**Middle aged adults**
Young adults – may read online articles	**Teenagers** – know more about technology

(2) Tick ✓ any group in the diagram above who might be an audience for this article and cross ✗ any who are not.

(3) Your ideas will need to consider the points of view held by your audience. Using your notes from above, complete 🖉 this table with appropriate ideas.

Audience	Point of view and ideas
Senior citizens	Uninterested in technology – need advice and encouragement …

3 **How do I generate ideas to build towards a powerful conclusion?**

The evidence you choose to support your ideas can help strengthen your argument and lead it to a powerful conclusion.

1 Your evidence will be more powerful if it is amusing, shocking or very authoritative. Look at these examples.

POV	Idea	Evidence	Conclusion
Modern technology is a powerful tool in the fight against ageing.	Using technology can help in the fight to keep the body fit.	Amusing anecdote that creates powerful image – taught grandmother online games; she's now got her bowls club out hunting for Pikachu!	Younger people owe it to the older generation to support them with modern technology.

Add 🖉 two more ideas and pieces of evidence that will direct the audience towards the conclusion.

Idea	Evidence

2 Your ideas may also need evidence to help overcome your audience's negativity about your point of view. Come up 🖉 with some ideas and evidence that would be powerful enough to overcome these objections.

a Older person who is uninterested in technology, feels it is a young person's arena:

Idea: ....

....

Evidence: ....

....

b Young adult who sees no benefit in helping the elderly get online:

Idea: ....

....

Evidence: ....

....

Sample response

To generate powerful ideas for your transactional writing you will need to:

- establish a powerful overall point of view that suits the purpose
- develop ideas that take into account the audience's needs, interests and views
- use evidence that leads to a firm conclusion.

Now look again at the exam-style writing task that you saw at the start of this unit.

Exam-style question

Write an article for a national newspaper about the benefits of modern technology for older people.

You could write about:

- what types of technology are available
- how technology will make their lives easier
- where to get help with modern technology

as well as any other ideas you might have.

(40 marks)

Look at this student's planning for the task.

POV: Keeps them in touch with the modern world.
Social networking – can keep up with relatives
Online shopping – every retailer now online, cheaper deals often available
Gaming – not just Pokemon and COD; whole world of classic games available
Conclusion: The world is modern – older people must join in.

1. Develop ✏ the ideas above to make them suitable for the wide audience of a national newspaper.

2. Add ✏ evidence that takes into account the views of the audience and directs them towards the conclusion.

Your turn!

You are now going to plan your response to this exam-style task.

Exam-style question

Write an article for a national newspaper about the benefits of modern technology for older people.

You could write about:

- what types of technology are available
- how technology will make their lives easier
- where to get help with modern technology

as well as any other ideas you might have.

(40 marks)

(1) What is your overall point of view? ✏️

....

....

....

....

(2) What ideas will suit your audience's needs, interests and views? Come up with three. ✏️

Idea 1: ....

....

Idea 2: ....

....

Idea 3: ....

....

(3) What evidence will direct your audience towards a firm conclusion? ✏️

....

....

....

....

....

....

....

....

Conclusion ....

....

....

Unit 2 Generating ideas – transactional writing   15

Review your skills

Check up

Review your response to the exam-style question on page 15. Tick ✓ the column to show how well you think you have done each of the following.

	Not quite ✓	Nearly there ✓	Got it! ✓
established a point of view that suits my purpose	☐	☐	☐
selected ideas to suit my audience	☐	☐	☐
generated ideas to build towards a powerful conclusion	☐	☐	☐

Look over all your work in this unit. Note 🖉 down the **three** most important things to remember when generating ideas for transactional writing.

1. ....

2. ....

3. ....

Need more practice?

Plan your response to the exam-style task below.

Exam-style question

Write an article for a newspaper, giving your views about reality television.

You could write about:

- the types of reality television show
- the effect reality television has on people's lives
- your views on reality television

as well as any other ideas you might have.

(40 marks)

How confident do you feel about each of these **skills?** Colour 🖉 in the bars.

1 How do I establish a point of view that suits my purpose? ☐☐☐☐

2 How do I select ideas to suit my audience? ☐☐☐☐

3 How do I generate ideas to build towards a powerful conclusion? ☐☐☐☐

③ Structuring your ideas – imaginative writing

This unit will help you learn how to structure your ideas for an imaginative writing task. The skills you will build are to:

- shape your ideas for maximum impact

- manipulate your ideas to create impact

- create an engaging opening and an ending with impact.

In the exam, you will be asked to tackle writing tasks such as the one below. This unit will prepare you to write your own response to this question.

Exam-style question

Write about a time when you, or someone you know, told a lie.

Your response could be real or imagined.   (40 marks)

The three key questions in the **skills boosts** will help you to structure your ideas for an imaginative writing task.

① **How do I shape my narrative for maximum impact?**   ② **How do I manipulate the structure of my ideas for impact?**   ③ **How do I start and end my narrative for greatest impact?**

Look at one student's plan on the next page.

Exposition:	Describe classroom, bored students, oppressive heat, restricted by jackets/ties.
Rising action:	Tension created as teacher comes in, asks 'Who did it?', waits for somebody to own up. Don't describe 'crime'.
Climax:	Describe feelings of hatred for Tom, who is good looking, cool, has everything and is loved by everybody. Describe own appearance as lonely geek. Put hand up and shout 'Tom!'
Falling action:	Tom taken away, then suspended, then excluded from school. Falls into petty crime, then drug addiction while I go to university and climb career ladder.
Resolution:	See Tom begging in town, walk past him quickly. Finally reveal that I did 'it'.

(1) What techniques has this student used to create impact? List ✐ two.

....

....

(2) The narrative takes a chronological approach. How could the structure be changed to create greater impact? ✐

....

....

....

....

....

....

(3) The events of the story seem to have had little impact on the narrator. How could the resolution be changed to create more character development? ✐

....

....

....

....

....

....

(4) Plan this story to add greater impact.

1 How do I shape my narrative for maximum impact?

To create maximum impact with your imaginative writing, it is important to focus on character and plot development. To do this you should:

- avoid unnecessary plot complications
- focus on one or two main characters and show development.

① Look at this plan for the exam-style question from page 17. It uses a five-part narrative structure and has a lot of complicated detail.

Exposition: Wake up in chalet, have breakfast with best friend who warns me to own up to lie, ignore him, find ski equipment, give safety talk to group of beginners, etc. Attractive girl falls on way to cable car, get to her before good-looking French instructor, help her up and hope she sees me as a 'hero'.	
Rising action: Have argument with French instructor about who skis first, rush to edge of slope to show off, launch myself over edge. Attractive girl very impressed. Fly through air with group all gasping behind me.	
Climax: Ski too fast down slope, get out of control, narrowly avoid hitting group of young children who are all skiing well, fly off piste into snow bank. Lose control completely, finally admit lie – am not instructor; have only skied on dry slope at home.	

Falling action:

Resolution:

Rewrite and finish the plan above.

ⓐ First, focus on the central plot and main character development.

ⓑ Then discard any unnecessary characters.

2 How do I manipulate the structure of my ideas for impact?

To add further impact to your imaginative writing you can manipulate the structure of your narrative.

(1) Read these extracts from the narrative. Which of these could be used as an opening to the story? Tick ✐ your choice. Then write ✐ one sentence explaining your choice.

☐	The climax	Racing down the slope I really did see my life pass before my eyes. I also saw, and narrowly avoided annihilating, a crocodile of young French skiers.
☐	The falling action	Opening one eye slowly I focused first on my bodily sensations. A raging headache. A terrible thirst. And a massive plaster cast on my left leg. I shifted my focus to the room I was in.
☐	The resolution	I'll never tell a lie again. The crash cost me my job, my best friend and all of my savings.

....

....

....

(2) You can also manipulate structure by switching between tenses. For instance, you could begin a narrative in the present tense, then switch to the past tense for a flashback. Read the resolution below, then plan ✐ the next two parts of this narrative using two different tenses to create impact.

The resolution	Now I stand at the very back of the crocodile of beginners. Crouching down is hopeless; I'll just have to own up to my lie. My turn approaches. I take a deep breath. I finally say it out loud: 'I can't ski!'

3 How do I start and end my narrative for greatest impact?

A successful piece of imaginative writing needs to hook a reader from the very start. It should have an opening that establishes the genre, and a convincing ending that creates a strong final impression.

1 Look at these four openings to the story about a lie.

A	Dialogue – gives readers immediate ideas about characters	'I'm scared. What do we do now?' Shadows played across Ellie's face as she whispered her fears. 'Keep still and I'll get you out. I'm a police officer.' The lie, sliding so naturally from his mouth, was such balm to the girl's panic that he almost believed it himself.	☐
B	Create an enigma – makes readers want answers	It was, after all, only a very small lie. People took so little notice of me that my tall tales were usually forgotten before the next round of beers. But this time ...	☐
C	Create a mood with description	The house sits still and silent, squatting low as if to keep out the stinging embrace of the winter storm. I hesitate at the threshold, allowing the darkness to cloak the truth for just a few seconds more.	☐
D	Create immediate conflict or danger	She froze. Twenty years had passed since her last sight of him. To talk to him now, after all she had done, was to cross over into a different world. One where he would finally have to be told the truth.	☐

a Which opening creates the most dramatic mood? Tick ✓ one, then write ✐ a sentence to explain the reason for your choice.

....

....

....

b Which opening would create the most amusing narrative? Cross ✗ one, then write ✐ a sentence explaining how you would continue the narrative.

....

....

....

2 Now look at three ways in which events can develop at the end of a story.

☐ 1. With all conflict resolved – often with a lesson learned by the main character.

☐ 2. On a cliffhanger – the fate of the character or characters is left in the balance.

☐ 3. With a plot twist – an unexpected event changes everything.

Tick ✓ the one type of ending that you think would most suit opening D above. Then write ✐ one or two sentences explaining how you would end the narrative.

....

....

....

....

Sample response

To structure imaginative writing successfully you should:
- avoid unnecessary plot complications and a large cast of characters
- manipulate the narrative structure for maximum impact
- plan an opening that establishes the genre and hooks the reader
- plan a strong and convincing ending.

Look at this exam-style writing task, which you saw at the start of the unit.

Exam-style question

Write about a time when you, or someone you know, told a lie.

Your response could be real or imagined.

(40 marks)

1 Look at this story plan.

Exposition	Rising action	Conflict	Climax	Resolution
I pretend I know a secret recipe for a new sweet so that I can get a job in a sweet factory.	Start work at factory, make friends with owner's son who tells me they will have to close soon without new recipe.	I stay up all night at the factory trying to discover new sweet idea. I panic and overcook some sugar, which causes a fire.	My friend is burned in the fire and thinks it is all his fault. He thinks I had a recipe that was lost in the fire.	I tell my friend the truth and he forgives me, saying that we will work on a new recipe together.

a Write 🖉 a stronger and more convincing idea for the ending of the story.

....

....

....

b Think how you could manipulate the structure to create more impact. Write 🖉 one or two sentences explaining your ideas.

....

....

....

....

c Write 🖉 the first two sentences of an opening that would hook the reader.

....

....

....

Your turn!

You are now going to plan your response to this exam-style task.

Write about a time when you, or someone you know, told a lie.

Your response could be real or imagined.   (40 marks)

① Come up with 🖉 some initial ideas.

② Develop 🖉 your ideas into a five-part structure. Avoid unnecessary plot complications and large casts of characters.

1	2	3	4	5

③ Now re-number 🖉 your structure into an order that will have the greatest impact on a reader.

④ Write 🖉 one or two opening sentences that signal your genre and hook your reader at the start of your narrative.

Review your skills

Check up

Review your response to the exam-style question on page 23. Tick ✓ the column to show how well you think you have done each of the following.

	Not quite ✓	Nearly there ✓	Got it! ✓
shaped my narrative for maximum impact	☐	☐	☐
manipulated the structure of my ideas for impact	☐	☐	☐
started and ended my narrative for greatest impact	☐	☐	☐

Look over all of your work in this unit. Note down ✐ the three most important ingredients for a successfully structured piece of imaginative writing.

1. ....

....

2. ....

....

3. ....

....

Need more practice?

Plan your response to the exam-style question below.

Exam-style question

Write about a time when you, or someone you know, visited a favourite relative.

Your response could be real or imagined.

(40 marks)

How confident do you feel about each of these **skills?** Colour ✐ in the bars.

1 How do I shape my narrative for maximum impact?

2 How do I manipulate the structure of my ideas for impact?

3 How do I start and end my narrative for greatest impact?

4 Structuring your ideas – transactional writing

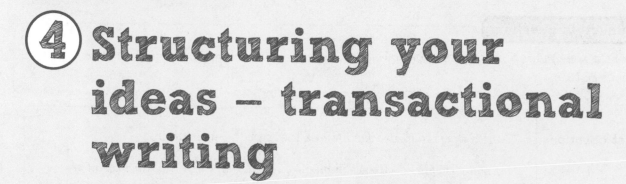

This unit will help you learn how to structure your ideas in the transactional writing task. The skills you will build are to:

• shape your ideas to create maximum impact

• plan an effective opening and link it to a conclusion

• sequence and develop your ideas.

In the exam, you will be asked to tackle writing tasks such as the one below. This unit will prepare you to write your own response to this question.

Exam-style question

Write an article for a newspaper advising parents how to help their children with the stress of exams.

You could write about:

• what causes the stress and how teenagers feel when stressed

• what practical help parents can give to their children

• where parents can go to get support and advice

as well as any other ideas you might have.

(40 marks)

The three key questions in the **skills boosts** will help you to structure your ideas in a transactional writing task.

 1 How do I shape my ideas?

2 How do I write an effective opening and conclusion?

3 How do I sequence and develop my ideas?

Look at one student's plan for a similar task on the next page.

Write a speech for a school assembly, giving your views about whether watching television is a waste of time.

Introduction	TV is a thief. It steals your life and leaves you fat and boring.
1	Too many channels, not enough quality, too easy to watch rubbish instead of educational programmes.
2	So many other worthier things to do – sport, reading, cinema, theatre.
3	TV watching is too passive; we have become a nation of couch potatoes.
4	Kills family life, nobody eats around a table; encourages unhealthy food choices.
5	Just a vehicle for advertising, much of which is damaging to people's (particularly children's) self-esteem.
6	Reality TV is biggest draw for young people; isn't even 'real'; creates unrealistic lifestyle aspirations; promotes idea that fame is important; creates a very judgemental society; ridicules people.
Conclusion	Perhaps TV is no longer the real thief? Have we all just swapped TV for the chains of social media?

1. Look carefully at the plan above, thinking about each of the areas below. Write (✐) one or two sentences commenting on each area, and then assess its effectiveness by awarding it a mark out of 5.

Ideas: are there enough ideas? Could any be discarded or combined to make the plan more concise?

....

....

....   /5

....

Opening and conclusion: will the opening fully engage a reader? Will the conclusion leave a lasting impression?

....

....

....   /5

....

Structure of ideas: is the sequence of ideas powerful or do changes need to be made? Is the sequence of ideas logical? Could they be sequenced more logically?

....

....

....   /5

....

How do I shape my ideas?

To make your transactional writing more effective, you need to use the most relevant and powerful of your ideas. To achieve this, you should:

- discard weak or less relevant ideas
- combine related ideas to make your writing more concise
- consider including some controversial ideas.

(1) Look at this student's plan for the exam-style question on page 25.

1. What causes the stress? Pressure from teachers/peers/social media; may get anxious or depressed, use statistics.

2. Parental pressure is an issue.

3. Feed them well but allow treats, make sure they sleep, etc.

4. Help them do a revision plan.

5. Give them a break from household chores; try not to nag about 'small stuff'.

6. Allow them to be moody/withdrawn – mention danger signs.

7. Be radical – stop them revising, encourage them to socialise, take them on holiday (better to face exams refreshed).

a Are there any points that are weak or too obvious? Mark them with a cross (✗).

b Could any points be combined to make the plan more concise? Mark with a tick (✓) those you can combine.

(2) Which point in the above plan is the most controversial? Write (✎) one or two sentences about why it is controversial and whether it would be effective.

....

....

....

....

....

....

(3) Think of another powerful controversial idea. (✎)

....

....

....

....

2 How do I write an effective opening and conclusion?

An effective introduction should make your views clear and instantly engage your audience. A conclusion should further emphasis your view and be powerful enough to leave a lasting impression.

① Look at these examples of openings and conclusions.

1 Start an anecdote	2 Use shocking or surprising facts/ statistics	3 Make a controversial statement	4 Use an analogy or metaphor
A week before his first A Level, my best friend Mike flew to Cyprus for a diving holiday.	Over 50 per cent of Oxbridge graduates admit to doing absolutely no revision before their GCSEs.	Exam stress? It's what every genius suffered from at the age of 16.	Helping a child with revision is like trying to spoon feed a baby tiger. Necessary, but dangerous.

A Refer back to anecdote	B End with a thought-provoking question	C End on a happy note	D End with a vivid image or warning
So, I hear you asking, how did my friend get on when he opened his results envelope? He passed with flying colours, obviously.	If all else fails, try asking them this simple question: Will the world end if they take a break for one night?	However unlikely it seems at the moment, the horror of exam season will pass.	Huddled into a corner, sobbing over a textbook and clutching a stub of pencil. Not the best way to face the exam season, is it?

ⓐ Which conclusion goes most effectively with which introduction? Join them ✏ with arrows.

ⓑ Which introduction and conclusion pair is the most powerful? Write ✏ two or three sentences explaining your choice.

....

....

....

....

② Now use one of the techniques above to write ✏ your own introduction and conclusion.

Introduction:...

....

....

Conclusion: ....

....

....

How do I sequence and develop my ideas?

To sequence your ideas effectively, you need to ensure your most powerful ideas are placed where they will have most impact.

(1) Below are two students' plans in response to this exam-style task.

> **Exam-style question**
>
> Write an article for a newspaper advising parents how to help their children with the stress of exams.

Student A	Student B
Plan	Plan
Intro: Anecdote about friend going on holiday.	Intro: Controversial comment about Bill Gates having done little revision.
1. Give obvious advice about eating well, getting exercise, taking breaks, etc.	1. Explain stress – caused by need to conform and compete, peer pressure, etc.
2. Explain pressure on teens that causes stress – from peers, teachers, social media.	2. Controversial idea – rather than revision, take a long-term approach, encourage entrepreneurship, etc.
3. Give less obvious advice about avoiding parental pressure.	3. Give advice about how to ease stress – eat well, spend time as a family, encourage exercise, etc.
4. Give controversial advice – think about easing the pressure by limiting revision, encouraging socialising, taking a last-minute holiday.	4. Final advice – trust children to work hard, avoid nagging, don't set unreasonable homework targets.
Conclusion: Return to anecdote.	Conclusion – Return to Bill Gates analogy.

Which student has planned the most effective sequence? Write ✐ about three sentences explaining your choice.

....

....

....

....

(2) Look again at the plan you thought was weaker. Think about where the controversial idea should be placed for maximum impact. Use the space below to experiment ✐ with a sequence that would make the plan more powerful.

Sample response

To effectively structure your transactional writing, you should consider:

- including a controversial idea
- using an introduction that instantly engages your reader
- writing a conclusion that leaves a lasting impression
- sequencing your ideas so that the most powerful ones have maximum impact.

You are now going to write your response to this exam-style task.

Exam-style question

Write a speech for a school assembly giving your views about whether watching television is a waste of time.

Use the activities below to help you identify your views and gather some strong ideas.

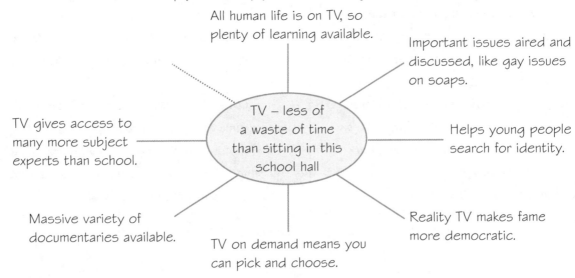

All human life is on TV, so plenty of learning available.

Important issues aired and discussed, like gay issues on soaps.

TV gives access to many more subject experts than school.

TV – less of a waste of time than sitting in this school hall

Helps young people search for identity.

Massive variety of documentaries available.

TV on demand means you can pick and choose.

Reality TV makes fame more democratic.

(1) Add 🖉 a controversial idea to the plan to make your speech more powerful.

(2) Cross out ⊗ any weak or irrelevant ideas. Use the remaining points to write 🖉 a more concise plan.

(3) Use this space to write 🖉 a powerful conclusion.

Your turn!

You are now going to write your response to this exam-style task.

Exam-style question

Write an article for a newspaper advising parents how to help their children with the stress of exams.

You could write about:

- what causes the stress and how teenagers feel when stressed
- what practical help parents can give to their children
- where parents can go to get support and advice

as well as any other ideas you might have.

(40 marks)

Use this space to plan 🖉 a powerful response. Make sure you are ruthless with any weak or irrelevant ideas.

Review your skills

Check up

Review your response to the exam-style question on page 31. Tick ✓ the column to show how well you think you have done each of the following.

	Not quite ✓	Nearly there ✓	Got it! ✓
shaped my ideas	☐	☐	☐
written an effective opening and conclusion	☐	☐	☐
sequenced and developed my ideas	☐	☐	☐

Look over all of your work in this unit. Note down ✐ three things that you should remember to do when structuring a transactional text.

1. ....

2. ....

3. ....

Need more practice?

Plan your response to the task below.

Exam-style question

Your local newspaper is holding a speech-writing competition and entries are invited with the title, 'School is cruel'. Write a speech as your competition entry.

In your speech you could:

- give examples of ways in which school might be considered 'cruel'
- describe who might find school cruel and why
- explain your ideas about whether school is cruel

as well as any other ideas you might have.

(40 marks)

How confident do you feel about each of these **skills?** Colour ✐ in the bars.

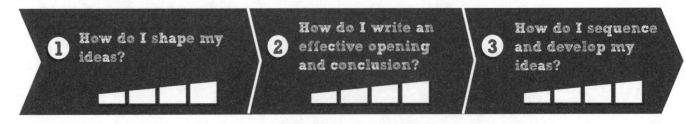

1. How do I shape my ideas?

2. How do I write an effective opening and conclusion?

3. How do I sequence and develop my ideas?

(5) Cohesion – making it clear

This unit will help you learn how to give your writing cohesion: guiding the reader through your ideas by linking them clearly and fluently. The skills you will build are to:

- use a broad range of discourse markers as signposts in your writing
- structure your paragraphs to link your ideas
- signpost and develop your ideas without repetition.

In the exam, you will be asked to tackle writing tasks such as the ones below. This unit will prepare you to write your own responses to these questions.

Paper 1

Exam-style question

Write about a time when you, or someone you know, made a serious mistake.

Your response could be real or imagined.   **(40 marks)**

Paper 2

Exam-style question

Write a letter to the Prime Minister, suggesting improvements to the current education system.

In your letter you could:

- state what the current education system is like for students
- explain why changes should be made to the education system
- make suggestions about how the education system could be changed

as well as any other ideas you might have.   **(40 marks)**

The three key questions in the **skills boosts** will help you to achieve cohesion in your writing by linking your ideas fluently and clearly.

1 How do I guide the reader through my writing?

2 How do I structure paragraphs to link my ideas?

3 How do I develop my ideas without repeating myself?

Look at extracts from one student's answers to the tasks on the next page.

Paper 1

Exam-style question

Write about a time when you, or someone you know, made a serious mistake.

☐ *You might think that my mistake is not that serious. My mistake involved helping a member of my family, it involved a charitable cause that involves animals, it made a family member very rich and my mistake ended happily for all concerned. Especially for my aunt.*

☐ *My aunt is the only woman I know who still wears gloves in the house, who still calls lunch 'luncheon' and who still expects a handwritten thank-you note for every carefully chosen, but completely unwanted, Christmas gift.*

1 Read the students' paragrahs above. Tick ✐ the paragraph that uses repetition more effectively. Write ✐ one sentence explaining the effect of the repetition.

....

....

2 Now consider the other paragraph. Try rewriting it ✐ with more fluency and greater impact.

....

....

....

....

....

Paper 2

Exam-style question

Write a letter to the Prime Minister, suggesting improvements to the current education system.

First, I believe our schools have degenerated into nothing more than exam factories. For example, secondary students spend the majority of their time cramming for tests; therefore there is no time for artistic pursuits. In addition, the constant round of in-school testing leads to unacceptable levels of stress and, for some students, it can lead to serious depression. Accordingly, students become so over-tested that they are subsequently unable to perform to their maximum potential in their GCSEs.

3 Annotate ✐ the paragraph above giving advice to the student on how it could be improved to make it more fluent.

How do I guide the reader through my writing?

You will need a wide range of discourse markers to develop your ideas into fluent arguments. However, too many 'stand alone' discourse markers can make an answer seem formulaic.

1 Paragraph B develops ideas using integrated discourse markers that don't interrupt the flow. Underline (A) the words or phrases that have been used in Paragraph B to replace the formulaic discourse markers in Paragraph A.

A

Additionally, our current system, which encourages over-testing, leads to serious mental health issues. For example, every year over 30 teenagers are treated for stress and depression during the exam season. While this does not seem an enormous number, it does however show that it is an issue that should not be ignored.

B

Mental health issues are another serious consequence of our current system's encouragement of over-testing. This is evidenced by the 30 or more teenagers who are treated for stress and depression every exam season. Not a high number compared to the overall number taking exams, but significant enough not to ignore.

Discourse markers like these can be useful for guiding your reader through your arguments.

- besides
- in spite of
- hence
- in my experience
- what is more
- the fact that
- indeed
- take, for example
- yet
- to put it simply
- resulting in
- it may seem that
- significantly
- as evidenced by
- despite

2 Look at this answer to the Paper 2 exam-style question on page 34. Underline (A) the words or phrases used to signpost the reader through the ideas in this paragraph.

In spite of the fact that our students take an ever-increasing number of exams, achievement is not improving rapidly enough. English students take an average of ten GCSEs, yet many still fail to secure five at a C grade or above. What is more, their lowest grades are often in English and Maths, hence there is an increasing need for additional help with these key subjects in sixth-form colleges.

3 Join (✎) the following ideas together into a fluent argument using a range of discourse markers.

All emphasis is on academic subjects.

No longer any time in the curriculum for arts.

Artistic and creative subjects good for developing personal expression.

Students who take a balanced mix of academic and artistic subjects suffer less stress.

....

....

....

....

....

....

2 How do I structure paragraphs to link my ideas?

It is important to link the beginning of a new paragraph with the one before it. You can link by:

- ending a paragraph with a sentence that leads *forward* to the next paragraph, or
- starting a new paragraph in a way that links *back* to the previous paragraph.

(1) Look at this extract from a student's response.

Exam-style question

Write about a time when you, or someone you know, made a serious mistake.

> *Especially for my aunt.*
>
> *My aunt is the only woman I know who still wears gloves in the house, who still calls lunch 'luncheon' and who still expects a handwritten thank-you note for every carefully chosen, but completely unwanted, Christmas gift. One word from her can turn the air at a family dinner into ice; not even my father dares to cross her.*
>
> *It was at a family dinner that the seed of my mistake was first sown …*

a Underline Ⓐ where the paragraphs have been linked by leading forward or linking back.

b Finish 🖊 the third paragraph and link it to the first line of a fourth.

....

....

....

....

....

....

(2) Transactional writing can be linked in the same way. Read this paragraph.

> *English students take an average of ten GCSEs, yet many still fail to secure five at a C grade or above. What is more, their lowest grades are often in English and Maths, hence there is an increasing need for additional help with these key subjects in sixth-form colleges.*

Write 🖊 a final sentence for this paragraph that looks forward to a paragraph about how 18-year-olds lack the literacy skills necessary to enter the jobs market.

....

....

....

....

....

③ How do I develop my ideas without repeating myself?

In any piece of writing, there will be key ideas that you will need to keep referring to. To avoid repeating yourself you will need to think about **synonyms** and **reference chains**.

> **Synonyms:** words or phrases with a similar meaning
> **Reference chain:** reference to the same idea without repeating it

① Look at this extract from one student's response to the Paper 2 exam-style task on page 33. Rewrite 🖉 the paragraph, making it more fluent by using synonyms to replace any repetition.

> Some students feel that schools have degenerated into nothing more than testing factories. Students spend day after day cramming for tests, teachers spend evening after evening marking tests, leaving no time for artistic pursuits. Constant testing means students are so over-tested that many students are unable to perform to their maximum potential for important tests such as GCSEs.

....

....

....

....

....

....

....

....

② Now look at this extract and consider how clear it is. Rewrite 🖉 these sentences, keeping the fluency but removing any ambiguity.

> **Remember:** when using reference chains make it very clear exactly what is being referred to.

> My hand shook as I held the envelope and remembered my promise of the night before. It was small, and to most people, completely inconsequential. But to me it meant the difference between life and death. My fingers felt like ice as I ripped it open.

....

....

....

....

....

....

....

....

....

Unit 5 Cohesion – making it clear 37

Sample response

To make your writing as clear and fluent as possible you should:

- use a wide range of integrated discourse markers
- link your ideas across paragraphs
- avoid repetition by using synonyms or reference chains.

Now look at this exam-style writing task, which you saw at the start of the unit.

Exam-style question

Write a letter to the Prime Minister, suggesting improvements to the current education system.

In your letter you could:

- state what the current education system is like for students
- explain why changes should be made to the education system
- make suggestions about how the education system could be changed

as well as any other ideas you might have.

(40 marks)

Look at this sample answer.

First, I believe that we need to open up a debate about the purpose of education. For instance, is education intended to impart knowledge, or is education's purpose merely to prepare children for work? Education for its own sake would mean children spending more time studying the arts. Additionally, children would need to be allowed to follow their interests rather than following a rigid curriculum.

Second, we need to consider the lack of physical education in schools.

(1) How would you improve the fluency and clarity of this writing?

a Underline (A) any parts of the text that you feel could be expressed more fluently, or that need to be more cohesive.

b Rewrite (✏) the text by:
- using a wide range of integrated discourse markers
- avoiding repetition.
- linking the two paragraphs

....

....

....

....

....

....

....

....

Your turn!

Choose one of the two exam-style tasks that you saw at the beginning of this unit.

Paper 1

Exam-style question

Write about a time when you, or someone you know, made a serious mistake.

Your response could be real or imagined. (40 marks)

Paper 2

Exam-style question

Write a letter to the Prime Minister, suggesting improvements to the current education system.

In your letter you could:

- state what the current education system is like for students
- explain why changes should be made to the education system
- make suggestions about how the education system could be changed

as well as any other ideas you might have. (40 marks)

(1) Write ✐ the first two paragraphs of your response, focusing on the way in which you guide the reader through your ideas. Your ideas should be clear and fluent.

....
....
....
....
....
....
....
....
....
....
....
....
....
....
....
....

(2) Read through your work. Underline Ⓐ where you have used integrated discourse markers. Correct ✐ any repetition or unclear reference chains.

Review your skills

Check up

Review your response to the exam-style question on page 39. Tick ✓ the column to show how well you think you have done each of the following.

	Not quite ✓	Nearly there ✓	Got it! ✓
guided the reader through my writing	☐	☐	☐
structured paragraphs to link my ideas	☐	☐	☐
developed my ideas without repeating myself	☐	☐	☐

Look over all of your work in this unit. Note down ✏ three techniques that will make your writing clear and fluent

1. ....
2. ....
3. ....

Need more practice?

You could try another exam-style task.

Exam-style question

Write a report for your local council about the facilities available in your local area for young people.

In your report you could:

• state what is available at the moment for teenagers
• explain what is right/wrong with the facilities
• suggest how current facilities could be improved

as well as any other ideas you might have.

(40 marks)

How confident do you feel about each of these **skills?** Colour ✏ in the bars.

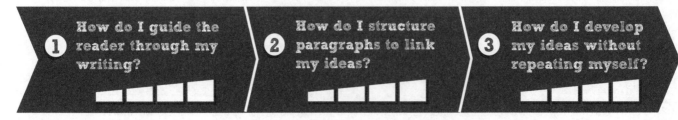

1 How do I guide the reader through my writing?

2 How do I structure paragraphs to link my ideas?

3 How do I develop my ideas without repeating myself?

(6) Making your meaning clear – sentences

This unit will help you express your ideas clearly and precisely. The skills you will build are to:

- use single-clause sentences with carefully chosen verbs and nouns
- experiment with clause positioning within sentences
- use semi-colons and colons to express ideas clearly.

In the exam, you will be asked to tackle writing tasks such as the ones below. This unit will prepare you to write your own response to one of these questions.

Paper 1

Exam-style question

Write about a time when you, or someone you know, received good news.

Your response could be real or imagined.   **(40 marks)**

Paper 2

Exam-style question

Write an article for a magazine exploring the importance of winning.

In your article you could:

- write about different types of winning
- describe the advantages of winning or having winners
- consider whether winning is always important

as well as any other ideas you might have.   **(40 marks)**

The three key questions in the **skills boosts** will help you to make your meaning clear.

1 How do I use single-clause sentences to clarify my meaning?

2 How do I experiment with sentence structure to clarify my meaning?

3 How do I use advanced punctuation to clarify my meaning?

Look at the extracts from two students' answers to the tasks on the next page.

Read the exam-style questions and the opening paragraphs.

Paper 1

Exam-style question

Write about a time you, or someone you know, received good news.

> I crashed the car when she told me. It was an ordinary day. We were just in the car park at the shopping centre, waiting for a space to come free. Maria was humming lazily to a tune on the radio. I was drumming my fingers impatiently on the steering wheel.

(1) What mood is created by the sentence structure? Write 🖉 one sentence explaining your view.

....

....

....

(2) Rewrite 🖉 one sentence to create more tension.

....

....

Paper 2

Exam-style question

Write an article for a magazine exploring the importance of winning.

> I always want to win and it doesn't matter whether I am playing a board game, taking a test at school or running the 100 metres. Life is a game for winners, and losers are just people who haven't worked hard enough to achieve their goals. Success is out there for everybody and you just have to find that one single thing you excel at.

(3) One sentence would be better expressed as a **single-clause sentence** to make the student's feelings even clearer.

> Single-clause sentence: sentence with one subject and one verb

a Find and underline Ⓐ that sentence.

....

....

b Write 🖉 the single-clause sentence here.

....

....

(4) Circle Ⓐ one other sentence in the paragraph. Then experiment with writing 🖉 a different structure for it.

....

....

42   Unit 6 Making your meaning clear – sentences

How do I use single-clause sentences to clarify my meaning?

Single-clause sentences can be used to summarise or emphasise information. They can also be used to create a particular atmosphere such as tension or humour.

(1) Look at these opening paragraphs from answers to the Paper 1 exam-style question on page 41.

> 'I've won the lottery.' I crashed the car when I heard her. It had started out as such an ordinary day. We were just edging towards the barrier at the shopping centre car park, waiting for a space to become free.

> I nearly didn't hear her. It was just an ordinary day. We were edging towards the barrier at the shopping centre car park, waiting for a space to become free when she dropped her bombshell. 'I've won the lottery.' I crashed the car when I realised what she'd said.

> I crashed the car. That's how shocked I was. It was just an ordinary day until that point. We were edging towards the barrier at the shopping centre car park, waiting for a space to become free. 'I've won the lottery,' she said.

Which paragraph uses single-clause sentences to best express the surprise felt by the narrator?

Tick 🖉 one. Explain 🖉 your choice. ....

....

....

(2) Consider these sentences from an answer to the Paper 2 exam-style question on page 41.

> I always want to succeed at everything.

> I always want to come first.

> I want to win.

> To ensure your single-clause sentences are effective, use carefully chosen nouns and verbs, and modify the verb only if you are sure it is necessary.

Tick ✓ the sentence that is most effective at expressing the view that winning is important.

Now explain 🖉 your choice. ....

....

....

(3) Write 🖉 two more single-clause sentences you could use at the start of an article about winning.

Sentence 1: ....

....

....

Sentence 2: ....

....

....

2 How do I experiment with sentence structure to clarify my meaning?

Changing the construction of a sentence can change the effect it creates.

(1) Look at these responses arguing that winning is not always important. In each one the clauses have been arranged in a different format.

> Life, many people say, is a game for winners and, if you're not a winner, you're a loser who hasn't tried hard enough. They could not be more wrong.

> If you're not a winner, you're a loser who hasn't tried. Life is, after all, a game for winners. Or so they say.

Tick ✓ the most effective version. Write ✏ one or two sentences explaining your choice.

....

....

....

....

(2) Experiment ✏ below with adverbials and adverbial phrases to alter the emphasis of this idea:

> Winning is necessary to prevent the loss of untapped human talent.

The emphasis of a sentence can be changed by altering the position of the adverbial. For example:
- Unfairly, those who come last are often considered to be losers.
- Those who come last are often unfairly considered to be complete losers.

Unfortunately	
Occasionally	
Without a doubt	

(3) Look at the same sentence with another clause added.

> Winning is necessary to prevent the loss of untapped human talent that will never surface without an element of competition.

Experiment ✏ with the meaning of this sentence on a separate piece of paper. Try:
- altering the position of the clauses
- adding adverbials or adverbial phrases
- using two separate sentences with/without adverbials.

3 How do I use advanced punctuation to clarify my meaning?

Using punctuation such as **colons** and **semi-colons** can make your transactional writing more fluent and concise. It can also add dramatic effects to your imaginative writing if used sparingly.

Colons: punctuation used between two main clauses for explanation or development. For example, the second clause in these sentences explains or develops the first:

- That is the secret to winning at any game: have some patience.
- I know how I'm going to handle this news: I'm going to face it head on.
- After extensive research, the study came to a conclusion about competitive sport: it was essentially damaging to children's development.

Semi-colons: punctuation used to balance complementary or contrasting points. For example:

- Some people will try to win at all costs; others are happy to come second.
- Alex sank back into the chair and laughed heartily; I just cringed.
- Unfortunately, the mistake wasn't Jesse's; it was mine.

① Add ✐ a complementary or contrasting point to complete these sentences.

My wife hates my obsession with winning; ....

....

....

Society needs winners; ....

....

....

I told him I would die rather than admit my mistake; ....

....

....

② Develop ✐ this sentence by using a colon and adding an explanation.

Having been both a winner and a loser, I have come to this conclusion: ....

....

....

③ Come up with ✐ a sentence that uses a colon in front of a short list.

....

....

....

....

....

....

....

Colons can also be very effective in front of a short list.

- This is how it works: I train hard, I focus hard, I win.
- There were only three ways I was going to get out of this mess: lie, cheat or run for my life.

Sample response

To ensure your meaning is clear you should:

- use some carefully crafted single-clause sentences to emphasise key ideas or create a particular atmosphere
- experiment with clause and adverbial positioning within your sentences
- use advanced punctuation to create specific effects.

Now look at this exam-style writing task, which you saw at the start of the unit.

Exam-style question

Write an article for a magazine exploring the importance of winning.

In your article you could:

- write about different types of winning
- describe the advantages of winning or having winners
- consider whether winning is always important

as well as any other ideas you might have.

(40 marks)

Look at this extract from one student's response.

> Just for one moment, stop what you are doing and imagine that the world contains no element of competition, no arena where you can be number one, no stadium full of people who will cheer your progress or applaud your success. Everybody is equal. It sounds wonderful. No losers, no disappointment, no failure. You might long for such a society. However, it would not suit my intensely competitive nature. I always want to win. It doesn't matter whether I am playing a board game, taking a test at school or running the 100 metres.

(1) How could the structure and punctuation of these sentences be improved to give the writer's feelings about winning more emphasis? Redraft ✏ them in the space below.

....

....

....

....

....

....

....

....

....

....

....

....

Your turn!

Choose one of the two exam-style tasks that you saw at the beginning of this unit.

Exam-style question

Write about a time when you, or someone you know, received good news.

Your response could be real or imagined.   **(40 marks)**

Exam-style question

Write an article for a magazine exploring the importance of winning.

In your article you could:

- write about different types of winning
- describe the advantages of winning or having winners
- consider whether winning is always important

as well as any other ideas you might have.   **(40 marks)**

You are going to **plan** and **write** the first two or three paragraphs of your response, focusing on sentence structure.

(1) Make a plan ✎ in the box below.

(2) Now use a separate sheet of paper to write ✎ the first three paragraphs of your response, focusing on using:

- a few single-clause sentences with carefully chosen nouns and verbs
- a variety of sentence structures
- advanced punctuation for dramatic effect.

> Reading your work aloud will help you check whether your meaning is clear. Don't be afraid to experiment by writing more than one draft.

Review your skills

Check up

Review your response to the exam-style questions on page 47. Tick ✓ the column to show how well you think you have done each of the following.

	Not quite ✓	Nearly there ✓	Got it! ✓
used single-clause sentences to clarify my meaning	☐	☐	☐
experimented with sentence structure to clarify my meaning	☐	☐	☐
used advanced punctuation to clarify my meaning	☐	☐	☐

Look over all of your work in this unit. Note down ✐ three pieces of advice you would give to another student who is struggling with sentence structure and punctuation.

1. ....

....

2. ....

....

3. ....

....

Need more practice?

You could:

- finish your response to the task you started on page 47
- attempt to write three paragraphs in response to the other task on page 47.

How confident do you feel about each of these **skills?** Colour ✐ in the bars.

1 How do I use single-clause sentences to clarify my meaning?

2 How do I experiment with sentence structure to clarify my meaning?

3 How do I use advanced punctuation to clarify my meaning?

(7) Writing paragraphs and sentences to create impact

This unit will help you learn how to write paragraphs and sentences that create impact. The skills you will build are to:

- create specific effects by experimenting with sentence positioning within paragraphs
- create specific effects by experimenting with sentence structures
- use advanced punctuation to create specific effects within sentences.

In the exam, you will be asked to tackle writing tasks such as the ones below. This unit will prepare you to write your own response to one of these questions.

Paper 1

Exam-style question

Write about a time when you, or someone you know, took a stand about something.

Your response could be real or imagined..   (40 marks)

Paper 2

Exam-style question

Write a review for a national newspaper of an event or an attraction in your local area.

You could write about:

- an attraction such as a museum or theme park, or an event such as a concert or sporting competition
- what the event or attraction offers for visitors such as available food and facilities for families
- your experiences at the event or attraction

as well as any other ideas you might have.   (40 marks)

The three key questions in the **skills boosts** will help you to write paragraphs and sentences to create impact.

1 How do I structure my paragraphs to engage the reader?

2 How do I experiment with sentence structure to create impact?

3 How do I use advanced punctuation to create impact?

Look at extracts from one student's answers to the tasks above on page 50.

Paper 1

Write about a time when you, or someone you know, took a stand about something.

Sinking back into his favourite chair, beer and crisps to hand, Daniel kicked off his shoes and stretched out his toes towards to the warmth of the crackling fire. Rain battered against the windows, autumn leaves danced around the garden and the wind whistled its way through the trees. Daniel sighed with contentment.

Later – once he had taken a stand – he was to see that moment as his last oasis of calm.

Paper 2

Write a review for a national newspaper of an event or an attraction in your local area.

When I was seven, my parents bought me my first skateboard. It wasn't very expensive – they thought it would just be a weekend wonder. Like many people, they viewed skateboarding (or 'skate-riding' as my mother embarrassingly insisted on calling it) as a teenage hobby rather than a 'sport'. I didn't care what they called what I was doing: every spare moment I could snatch from homework and chores was spent outside on that board. I was hooked.

Now I'm the British under-21 champion and I have my local skateboarding park to thank for my success.

(1) Look closely at the structure of the paragraphs and sentences in both student responses. Annotate (✏️) any paragraph or sentence that you feel is effectively structured. In your annotations, note:

- where the writer has positioned key information
- how the sentences have been constructed to create impact
- how advanced punctuation has been used for effect.

① How do I structure my paragraphs to engage the reader?

It is possible to create impact by using short paragraphs or by withholding key information until the end of a longer paragraph.

① Look at this opening. It creates dramatic impact by withholding the key information about what 'it' is until the last sentence.

> I realised the time had come to make a stand when I saw it under my brother's bed. I opened the door to a familiar carpet of discarded food, empty bottles, rusting cans, sweaty clothes, and reeking trainers. Approaching gingerly, I slid on what might once, several months ago, have been a cheese and pickle sandwich. Skirting around an army of drawing pins scattered menacingly on the bedside rug I caught sight of it peeking out from under a duvet. This was the final straw: he was keeping a snake in his bedroom.

ⓐ Dramatic impact could also be created by keeping back some of the information. What information could be put into a later separate short paragraph? Underline Ⓐ your choices.

ⓑ Use your choices to create ✏ two different versions of a short paragraph.

Version 1: ....
....
....
....

Version 2: ....
....
....
....

② Look at the sentence ideas below for a paragraph about an attraction to be reviewed.

ⓐ Number ✏ the sentences to create a paragraph structure that would engage a reader.

ⓑ Experiment ✏ on a separate sheet of paper with writing a longer paragraph that withholds key information until the very end.

☐ Men in shorts despite the chill in the air.

☐ The summer beach in our market square.

☐ The great British seaside.

☐ Sandcastles, bright plastic buckets and spades, people struggling with the origami of deckchairs, hands sticky from candyfloss that melts in the mouth.

☐ Children grizzle with boredom; parents sigh with exasperation: the summer holidays are here.

2 How do I experiment with sentence structure to create impact?

How you choose to open and structure your sentences can alter their impact on a reader. Try reading your work aloud to assess the impact of your sentence structures.

1 Read this paragraph aloud. Notice how a rhythm is built up through the use of different sentence openings and differing sentence lengths.

> I was trapped: the snake was lying motionless between my feet. In front of me, only two feet away, was the door, but with a 6-foot snake at my feet, it might as well have been in a different country. Cold sweat broke out on my forehead as I inched forwards.

These sentences use a pronoun, a preposition and an adjective as openers. Add ✎ a final sentence to this paragraph, opening it with either an article (a, an, the) or a conjunction (if, although, because, when, while).

....

....

2 Now look at the impact created by adding and rearranging clauses within a sentence.

> I edged towards the door.   I edged silently forward, making my way towards the door.

> My eyes never left the beast as I edged silently and slowly towards the door.

> Slowly and silently I edged towards the door, fists clenched and eyes never leaving the beast.

a Experiment ✎ with the ideas in the final sentence by rearranging the clauses and adding one more.

....

....

....

b Underline Ⓐ the sentence (including your own) that has the most impact on a reader. Briefly explain ✎ your choice.

....

....

3 Experiment ✎ with two further single-clause sentences that would add impact to the paragraph you finished for question 1.

....

....

Minor sentences that are grammatically incomplete can add impact to your writing, particularly if used after a multi-clause sentence. For example: Shops and cafés line the market square; with the beach, composed of a belt of beautifully smooth white sand, found just beyond a strip of decking bordered on both sides by the type of old-fashioned stall you haven't seen since you were five. The real seaside? No: but not a bad copy.

3 How do I use advanced punctuation to create impact?

Advanced punctuation, such as dashes and brackets, can be used to add dramatic emphasis or even humour to your writing. As a general rule, use brackets if you want to draw attention to additional information and dashes if you want to create maximum effect. Be careful not to overuse them, though, because your work might appear clichéd and formulaic.

(1) Brackets must be used in pairs. They generally contain additional, but not essential, information.

> Hordes of people flock to the Square each day and the beach (which the Council tried to ban) is easily the most popular of the summer attractions.

Notice how this bracketed information is used to hint that the writer does not agree with the Council's views.

Add 🖉 a bracketed hint to the following sentence by using an arrow ⬆ and writing 🖉 the bracketed information above it.

> An excited crowd was at fever pitch as the bass guitarist came on stage and began the sound check.

(2) Dashes can be used to add extra, but not entirely necessary, information to a sentence. In this way they can act as an 'aside'.

> The annual cleaning of my brother's lair – which mainly involved cramming everything visible into black bags – hadn't yet taken place.

Notice how this 'aside' reveals more about the character of the narrator's brother.

Rewrite 🖉 the following sentence, adding an aside with dashes.

> Several years ago I decided to take a stand against my brother's vile and completely inexcusable behaviour.

....

....

(3) A single dash can be used instead of a colon to add dramatic impact.

> Sometimes I forget why I'm so frightened of pets – then I remember the tarantula.

> There was actually only one ingredient missing from our local seaside scene – the sea itself.

Use dashes or a single dash to add dramatic effect to the following sentence. Rewrite 🖉 it on the lines below.

> Beaches are the perfect setting for a romantic evening encounter.

....

....

Unit 7 Writing paragraphs and sentences to create impact   53

Sample response

To craft paragraphs and sentences that create impact you should consider:

- using carefully constructed short paragraphs
- the placement of key information in a longer paragraph
- varying the openings and structures of your sentences
- using carefully placed advanced punctuation such as dashes and brackets.

Now look at this exam-style writing task, which you saw at the start of the unit.

Exam-style question

Write about a time when you, or someone you know, took a stand about something. Your response could be real or imagined.

(40 marks)

> Deep breathing, positive mantras, assertive body language – this is Day One of 'Taking a Stand'. I've never been a very confident person; in fact, I often struggle to believe in myself and in my own abilities, particularly if I go against the flow of peer pressure and dare to be different. Yet, for a long time, it had been clear to me that somebody needed to do something. Why not me? Many of my friends – while they weren't actually prepared to stand beside me – at least encouraged me, urging me on with words of support, while others (including my own mother) thought I was mad to even think of taking them on.

(1) Read the paragraph aloud and listen to the rhythm of the sentences.

- Notice the sentences lengths and structures. Where and how is any impact created?
- Notice how key information has been withheld. Does this add drama and engage the reader?
- Notice whether punctuation been used to add impact.

Annotate (✐) the paragraph with your observations. Make any amendments you feel would increase the impact of the paragraph.

(2) Now add (✐) another short paragraph of no more than two sentences.

....

....

....

....

Your turn!

You are now going to write your response to one of these exam-style tasks.

Paper 1

Exam-style question

Write about a time when you, or someone you know, took a stand about something.

Your response could be real or imagined.   **(40 marks)**

Paper 2

Exam-style question

Write a review for a national newspaper of an event or an attraction in your local area.

You could write about:

- an attraction such as a museum or theme park, or an event such as concert or sporting competition
- what the event or attraction offers for visitors such as available food and facilities for families
- your experiences at the event or attraction

as well as any other ideas you might have.   **(40 marks)**

① Think about all the different ideas you might include in your response. Note them 🖉 in the space below.

② Now write 🖉 your response to your chosen task on paper, thinking about:
  - your sentence openings and structures
  - your paragraph length
  - the sequence of your ideas within your paragraphs
  - how to use advanced punctuation carefully and sparingly to add impact.

Unit 7 Writing paragraphs and sentences to create impact   **55**

Review your skills

Check up

Review your response to the exam-style question on page 55. Tick ✓ the column to show how well you think you have done each of the following.

	Not quite ✓	Nearly there ✓	Got it! ✓
used paragraph structure to create some impact	☐	☐	☐
experimented with sentence structure to create impact	☐	☐	☐
used advanced punctuation to create impact	☐	☐	☐

Look over all of your work in this unit. Note down 🖉 three ways to increase the impact of your sentences and paragraphs.

1. ....
....
2. ....
....
3. ....
....

Need more practice?

Tackle the other writing task on page 55.

Remember to focus on creating impact through your choice of sentence and paragraph structure, and through your careful use of advanced punctuation.

How confident do you feel about each of these **skills?** Colour 🖉 in the bars.

1 How do I structure my paragraphs to engage the reader?

2 How do I experiment with sentence structure to create impact?

3 How do I use advanced punctuation to create impact?

(8) Making your meaning clear – choosing precise vocabulary

This unit will help you learn how to select vocabulary to make your meaning clear.
The skills you will build are to:

- select vocabulary that supports your intentions and maintains an appropriate tone
- use abstract nouns and noun phrases effectively to achieve sophistication
- experiment with ambitious vocabulary to maintain clarity and concision.

In the exam, you will be asked to tackle writing tasks such as the ones below. This unit will prepare you to write your own response to one of these questions.

Paper 1

Exam-style question

Write about a time when you, or someone you know, were embarrassed.

Your response could be real or imagined. (40 marks)

Paper 2

Exam-style question

Write a letter to your local newspaper, giving your views about the way young people are portrayed in the media.

In your letter you could:

- outline the negative ways teenagers are presented in many newspapers and on TV
- list the types of contribution teenagers make to society, e.g. volunteering, mentoring, fundraising
- explain your views about teenagers and the way they are portrayed

as well as any other ideas you might have. (40 marks)

The three key questions in the **skills boosts** will help you to make your meaning clear by choosing precise vocabulary.

1. How do I select vocabulary to create the right tone?

2. How do I use abstract nouns?

3. How do I choose precise vocabulary for clarity and concision?

Look at the extracts from students' answers to the tasks, on the next page.

Paper 1

Write about a time when you, or someone you know, were embarrassed.

> I was mortified. My discomfiture grew as I stood there exhaling ponderously. I could have yelled or shouted, agitated as I was, but my sense of humiliation was total. I could barely manage a whisper, so constrained were my throat and tongue. Alarmed at what the rows of formidable looking educators might be thinking, I inhaled deeply and made another attempt. But all was lost. Ignominy was heaped upon me that day – no other day could ever be as ruinous as the day I tried to narrate my life story to the whole school.

1 a Underline (A) any vocabulary choices you feel are particularly effective and circle (A) any that you feel could be improved.

b Note (✏) any vocabulary that you feel is over-elaborate beside the extract.

Paper 2

Write a letter to your local newspaper, giving your views about the way young people are portrayed in the media.

> According to some newspapers available at the present time – and your newspaper is the worst – most teenagers are inconsiderate, lazy, foul-mouthed yobs who spend their empty days hanging around on street corners, dropping litter and throwing things at passing cars. One in four juveniles has carried out an act of crime by the age of sixteen. Regular readers of both broadsheet and tabloid newspapers digest – and appear to be hugely entertained by – tales about teenagers who wreak havoc in their neighbourhoods: assaulting innocent, frail old ladies; stealing at knifepoint from local shops, restaurants and schools; committing untold criminal damage in public parks and shopping centres. Headlines abound about the '70 per cent of teenagers who smoke cannabis' and the '45 per cent who regularly binge drink'. Such scare stories are intended to shock in order to shift yet more newsprint. But do they tell the whole story of teenage life? What about the three out of four teenagers who live a life of blameless innocence?

2 Look at the highlighted vocabulary. Write (✏) a sentence explaining what tone it creates and how appropriate the tone is for the exam-style task. ....

....

....

3 Circle (A) two of the highlighted phrases that you think could be improved to make the writing clearer and more concise. Write (✏) your improved versions.

....

....

....

How do I select vocabulary to create the right tone?

Using an appropriate register for your writing will be important for both transactional and imaginative writing. It is tempting to use over-elaborate styles of vocabulary to create a sophisticated tone, but often a sparser style is more effective.

1 Look at this sentence written in response to the exam-style question on page 57.

> Contrary to the disturbing point of view portrayed by cheaper newspapers, in the majority of instances an examination of the way teenagers actually conduct themselves reveals that, on the whole, they live a fairly innocent and blameless existence.

a The sentence is over-elaborate, which makes the writer's point of view unclear. Experiment by replacing 📝 the highlighted phrases with clearer noun phrases and verbs from this table.

negative images	painted	tabloid press	live	exemplary lives
disturbing images	presented	red-top newspapers	lead their lives	
misleading images	peddled	the press	spend their time	

....

....

....

....

b Look at how this part of the sentence has been reworked.

> Despite what we see daily in the press, most young people live blameless lives.

Do you think the phrase 'young people' is more effective than the noun 'teenager'? Write 📝 a brief response here.

....

....

....

2 Circle Ⓐ the over-elaborate phrase in this sentence, then rewrite 📝 it using more precise vocabulary.

> Regular readers of your publication ought to be made aware of the exemplary life led by Ellie Hughes who, despite being incapacitated with frequent disabling bouts of an auto-immune disorder, spends the majority of her evenings and weekend mornings assisting at a local charity hospice for terminally ill children.

....

....

....

2 How do I use abstract nouns?

Replacing verbs and adjectives with abstract nouns or noun phrases can give your writing a more sophisticated style.

① Using abstract nouns in your imaginative writing can create a more sophisticated style, for instance:

She liked being alone.	She craved solitude.
I wasn't feeling very brave.	My courage deserted me/bravery was beyond me.
I could see the crowd was angry.	The animosity of the crowd was obvious.

a Experiment 🖉 with abstract nouns in these sentences.

Sam finally began to hope that this would stop her being so weak and timid.

....

....

I was going to be so embarrassed if I laughed at the wrong moment.

....

....

If I had known then what I know now, I might have been able to prevent myself from crying.

....

....

b Read your sentences aloud. Have you used too many abstract nouns? Correct 🖉 them to create appropriate tone. Use paper if you need more room.

② **Nominalisation** can give your transactional writing a more sophisticated tone. For example:

Nominalisation: using abstract nouns and noun phrases instead of verbs

Perhaps if people heard more about young people taking part in fundraising they might stop reading your stories about what crimes they commit.

Perhaps if the public received regular information about young people's participation in community charity events they might be less inclined to read your stories about their criminal activity.

Experiment 🖉 with nominalisation on the sentence below.

Be careful: overusing abstract nouns can make your writing sound stilted and pompous.

Nobody hears, for instance, about John Edwards, who walked miles for charity, getting serious blisters on both feet. He raised thousands of pounds.

....

....

....

③ How do I choose precise vocabulary for clarity and concision?

To ensure your writing is sophisticated, yet still clear, experiment with a wide variety of vocabulary.

① Look at this sentence written about teenagers.

> A brief look at the tabloids on any given day shows a lot of stories criticising young people.

a Underline Ⓐ an alternative vocabulary choice for each of the highlighted words in the sentence.

perusal	reveals	\<an\> abundance	tales	condemning
glance	exposes	plethora	articles	disparaging
examination	uncovers	wealth of	narratives	decrying

b Circle Ⓐ two of your choices and explain ✐ why they work better.

I chose .... because ....

....

I chose .... because ....

....

② Write ✐ a sentence or two explaining the positive contribution young people can make to society. Aim to use at least three ambitious words or phrases to precisely clarify your meaning.

....

....

....

....

③ **a** Draw lines ✐ to match these sentences with the effects they create.

Remember: in some instances simple word choices can work better.

> I deferred to his exalted status and acquiesced in his arcane schemes. After all, he was the boss.

> I yielded to his plots and schemes: he was the boss.

> He was the boss – I gave in.

> Suggests narrator only reluctantly gives in.

> Narrator had no other option.

> Narrator is sarcastic about his boss's plans and abilities.

b Write ✐ one more version that suggests the narrator is forced to follow 'his' plans.

....

....

....

....

Sample response

When making vocabulary choices, you should consider:

- the appropriate tone and register for the writing
- replacing verbs and adjectives with abstract nouns or noun phrases
- selecting vocabulary that expresses your ideas precisely.

Look at this Paper 2 exam-style writing task, which you saw at the start of the unit.

Exam-style question

Write a letter to your local newspaper, giving your views about the way young people are portrayed in the media.

In your letter you could:

- outline the negative ways teenagers are presented in many newspapers and on TV
- list the types of contributions teenagers make to society, e.g. volunteering, mentoring, fundraising
- explain your views about teenagers and the way they are portrayed

as well as any other ideas you might have.   (40 marks)

Now look at this extract from a student's response to it.

> Regular readers of your broadsheet could be forgiven for their belief that young people are feral creatures, loitering on street corners, spraying graffiti and spitting on pensioners. After all, these images sell papers. But are they the whole story?
>
> Positive narratives do exist. Many teenagers, Ali Brown is an example, relish the opportunities they are given to contribute to the society outside of their home and school. Ali, despite years of illness, defies the prevailing image of teenage delinquency on a regular basis. His actions come, not from a need for recognition or praise, but from a desire to make a difference to his local community.

(1) Annotate ✐ the paragraph with your observations about:
- the register created by the vocabulary choices
- the use of abstract nouns and noun phrases
- the mixture of ambitious vocabulary and simple phrases.

(2) Now add ✐ another paragraph of two or three sentences to add to the answer above.

....

....

....

....

Your turn!

You are now going to write your response to one of these exam-style tasks.

Paper 1

Exam-style question

Write about a time when you, or someone you know, were embarrassed.

Your response could be real or imagined. **(40 marks)**

Paper 2

Exam-style question

Write a letter to your local newspaper, giving your views about the way young people are portrayed in the media.

In your letter you could:

- outline the negative ways teenagers are presented in many newspapers and on TV
- list the types of contributions teenagers make to society, e.g. volunteering, mentoring, fundraising
- explain your views about teenagers and the way they are portrayed

as well as any other ideas you might have. **(40 marks)**

(1) Think about all the different ideas you might include in your response. Note them 🖉 in the space below.

(2) Now write 🖉 your response to your chosen task on paper, thinking about:
- an appropriate register
- your use of nouns and noun phrases to create a sophisticated tone
- vocabulary that will create precise and specific effects.

Review your skills

Check up

Review your response to the exam-style question on page 63. Tick ✓ the column to show how well you think you have done each of the following.

	Not quite ✓	Nearly there ✓	Got it! ✓
selected vocabulary to create the right tone	☐	☐	☐
used abstract nouns	☐	☐	☐
chose precise vocabulary for clarity and concision	☐	☐	☐

Look over all of your work in this unit. Note down ✐ three pieces of advice to give to a student who is struggling to produce sophisticated writing that is also clear and concise.

1. ....

....

2. ....

....

3. ....

....

Need more practice?

Tackle the other writing task on page 63.

Remember to focus on:

- achieving an appropriate register
- using nouns and noun phrases to create a sophisticated tone
- selecting vocabulary to express your ideas clearly, precisely and concisely.

How confident do you feel about each of these **skills?** Colour ✐ in the bars.

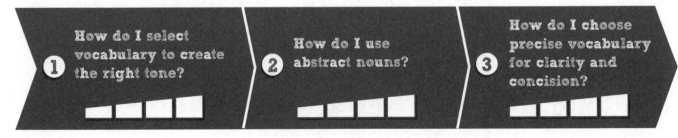

1. How do I select vocabulary to create the right tone?

2. How do I use abstract nouns?

3. How do I choose precise vocabulary for clarity and concision?

⑨ Selecting vocabulary for impact and effect

This unit will help you learn how to select vocabulary for impact and effect. The skills you will build are to:

- experiment with synonyms to achieve specific effects

- use figurative language for effect

- review the overall effect of vocabulary and figurative language.

In the exam, you will be asked to tackle writing tasks such as the ones below. This unit will prepare you to write your own response to one of these questions.

Paper 1

Exam-style question

Write about a time when you, or someone you know, found something hidden.

Your response could be real or imagined. **(40 marks)**

Paper 2

Exam-style question

Write the text for a speech giving your views about fast food.

You could choose to write about:

- the types of fast food available and where it can be bought

- the advantages and disadvantages of fast food

- your views about fast food

as well as any other ideas you might have. **(40 marks)**

The three key questions in the **skills boosts** will help you to select vocabulary for impact and effect.

 1 How do I explore vocabulary choices and their effects?

2 How do I use figurative language for effect?

 3 How do I ensure my vocabulary creates the right effect?

Look at the extracts from students' answers to the tasks on the next page.

Paper 1

> Rays of warm sunshine raced across the room as I flung back the curtains. Glistening and gleaming in the shimmer of the morning haze, the sea spread out before me like a silver carpet. Waves lapped gently at weathered outcrops of rock. An almost perfect semi-circle of fine, dark volcanic sand completed the unspoilt, Eden-like paradise.
>
> Later, armies of sunbathers would descend in pursuit of a small kingdom of beach to colonise. The seagulls would begin circling like hungry vultures looking for prey. Small children would babble and wail, wielding flimsy nets in rock pools, causing crabs to make frantic bids for freedom. But at that precise moment, before I found it, before I even knew it existed, the beach looked like heaven on earth.

(1) Read the extract aloud. Underline (A) two vocabulary choices you feel have an impact. Explain (✏) both choices.

Choice 1: ....

....

Choice 2: ....

....

(2) Now underline (A) a phrase or sentence that you feel lacks impact or is over-elaborate, and explain (✏) your choice.

....

....

Paper 2

> Where does our fast food come from? Most comes from factory-farmed animals. Your chicken nugget was probably kept in a small cage, standing in its own faeces, suffering from osteoporosis and joint pain, attacking other chickens because of the the lack of space. It may have had its beak cut off so it doesn't go crazy and peck its flesh. To keep the chickens from getting ill in these conditions, they are given antibiotics, which often end up in our food.
>
> Still want a chicken nugget? If that hasn't put you off, then consider what part of the chicken you might actually be eating. Forget that chicken breast you have on your plate every Sunday; your nugget is probably made from mechanically recovered meat – meat that is scraped from bones and made up of gristle, cartilage and fat.

(3) This extract lacks emotive impact. Select three of the highlighted words/phrases and experiment (✏) with more emotive vocabulary.

Choice 1: ....

....

Choice 2: ....

....

Choice 3: ....

....

1 How do I explore vocabulary choices and their effects?

One way to add impact to your writing is by exploring alternative vocabulary choices. But remember, your writing will be more effective if your vocabulary is chosen to suit your audience and your purpose.

1. Think carefully about which vocabulary best expresses your point of view. For instance, do you want to be descriptive, emotive, ambitious or very clear? For example, consider some other options for the verb 'put' in this sentence.

> Chickens are put into small crates and taken to the abattoir.

Sort the synonyms for 'put' below into the following groups by drawing lines from the word to the group.

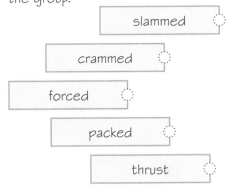
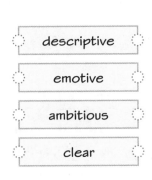
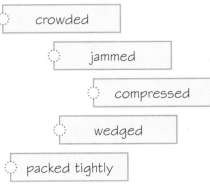

slammed

crammed

forced

packed

thrust

descriptive

emotive

ambitious

clear

crowded

jammed

compressed

wedged

packed tightly

2. Now consider these sentences.

A
> Your chicken nugget's journey started when a chicken – a chicken unlikely ever to have seen daylight – was slammed into a tiny crate for a short, but agonising, final journey: to the slaughter-house.

B
> The animals are thrust into wooden crates, packed so tightly they cannot move a muscle, and driven away for slaughter; a journey that can take several agonising hours.

a Which sentence is most suitable for a speech to a group of young people? Explain your choice.

....

....

b Annotate the highlighted phrases with your views about the impact of the word choices.

3. Consider this sentence from a speech to be given to parents. Does it need more impact? Rewrite it, selecting more effective vocabulary.

> Fast-food, if eaten on a regular basis, can be very harmful to the health of young children.

....

....

2 How do I use figurative language for effect?

Another way to add impact to your writing is through the use of carefully chosen figurative language.

1 Similes and metaphors can create powerful images for your audience. For example:

> Fast-food customers come to rely on their daily fix
> of grease and sugar.

What does this metaphor suggest about fast-food restaurants and their customers? Annotate 🖉 the sentence with your ideas.

2 Personification can be effective if used carefully. For example:

> Whenever I am about to enter a fast-food restaurant my health conscience creeps up behind me,
> taps me on the shoulder and says, 'What are you doing here?'

What type of audience would appreciate this sentence? Write 🖉 a sentence or two explaining your answer.

....

....

....

3 Imaginative writing has more impact if you use vocabulary to 'show' rather than 'tell'. Look at these extracts. Tick ✓ the extract that you think is more effective at creating tension. Annotate 🖉 your chosen extract with notes about the effect of the figurative language.

> ☐ I had goosebumps. There was a silence so thick I could
> hear every creak of the stairs. Beneath my feet I could
> feel the ice cold of the stone slabs. Darkness descended on
> the house and I held my breath.

> ☐ My skin prickled. Again and again the creak of the stairs
> pierced the silence. I froze, half squatting, half kneeling
> on the icy slabs. As darkness descended, the house waited
> and I, a frightened animal, held my breath.

3 How do I ensure my vocabulary creates the right effect?

It is important to review your vocabulary choices to ensure that the effect it creates suits both audience and purpose.

① Excessive modification of nouns and verbs can cause your work to lose clarity and concision. For example:

> The vast majority of British parents care very deeply about their children and it is therefore incredibly difficult to comprehend why they regularly overfeed them with huge amounts of terribly harmful substances that will seriously damage their offspring's long-term health and fitness.

Over-modification has made this sentence unwieldy. Make it concise by circling (Ⓐ) the modifications and rewriting (✏) the sentence with more effective vocabulary.

....

....

....

② Imaginative writing can suffer from overuse of figurative language. For example:

> The wind sang in the trees and the branches waved beneath an inky black sky. Thin, dingy rain spat and drizzled. From under an umbrella of dripping leaves I could see it – just out of my reach, a glistening jewel teasing me from the shadows. The bitter juice of fear filled my mouth as I stretched out my hand to grasp my prize.

Effective imaginative writing should have a distinct rhythm. Read this extract aloud several times and then cross through (✗) any language that you feel upsets the textual rhythm.

③ Transactional writing can suffer from overuse of language techniques. For example:

> Who in their right mind would feed their children fast food every day? According to a recent study, over 50 per cent of teenagers are now obese. Before stuffing your children full of greasy burgers, e-number-laden fizzy drinks and calorie-dense smoothies, remember that you are condemning them to a life of obesity. And obesity increases their risk of diabetes, heart attack, depression, liver failure and breathing difficulties. So remember, every time you give them a burger you are playing Russian Roulette with their future health.

What prevents this writing from having a sophisticated tone that would appeal to an adult audience? Write (✏) a sentence or two to explain.

....

....

....

....

Sample response

You should always review your vocabulary for impact and effect. To do this:

- read your work through and listen to the rhythm (does it sound effective?)

- have a critical look at your figurative language (is it over-elaborate?)

- think about your point of view (do your vocabulary choices fully support your ideas?).

Look at the exam-style writing task from Paper 2, then read part of the student's response.

Exam-style question

Write the text for a speech giving your views about fast food.

You could choose to write about:

- the types of fast food available and where it can be bought
- the advantages and disadvantages of fast food
- your views about fast food

as well as any other ideas you might have.

(40 marks)

> In the UK, at this very moment, hordes of children, some as young as three years old, are being force-fed the most appalling rubbish. Rubbish that fast-food restaurants everywhere dare to label as food. Rubbish that lazy parents across the land tell themselves is a proper meal. Rubbish that is fed to children so brainwashed that many think 'five a day' means five helpings of chicken nuggets.
>
> Towers of slimy burgers and mountains of greasy fries – followed by lakes of chemical-smelling fizzy drink. A sugar rush as potent and, some would argue, as damaging as heroin. What started as a treat when fast-food burgers and fries first hit our shores in the 1970s has now become the regular diet of an increasingly large number of Britain's children.

1 What is the writer's point of view in these paragraphs? Write ✐ a sentence or two to explain.

....

....

....

2 Circle Ⓐ five vocabulary choices in the extract that you feel are particularly effective. Annotate them ✐ with your ideas about why they are effective.

3 Look at the highlighted vocabulary in the first paragraph. Experiment by changing these choices ✐ to increase the impact.

Your turn!

You are now going to write your response to one of these exam-style tasks.

Paper 1

Exam-style question

Write about a time when you, or someone you know, found something hidden.

Your response could be real or imagined. **(40 marks)**

Paper 2

Exam-style question

Write the text for a speech giving your views about fast food.

You could choose to write about:

- the types of fast food available and where it can be bought
- the advantages and disadvantages of fast food
- your views about fast food

as well as any other ideas you might have. **(40 marks)**

① Plan 🖊 your response in this box.

② Now write 🖊 your response to your chosen task on paper. Think carefully about selecting, reviewing and improving vocabulary choices to help you achieve your intention.

Unit 9 Selecting vocabulary for impact and effect 71

Review your skills

Check up

Review your response to the exam-style question on page 71. Tick ✓ the column to show how well you think you have done each of the following.

	Not quite ✓	Nearly there ✓	Got it! ✓
explored vocabulary choices and their effects	☐	☐	☐
used figurative language for effect	☐	☐	☐
ensured my vocabulary created the right effect	☐	☐	☐

Look over all your work in this unit. Note down 🖉 the three most important things to remember when selecting vocabulary for impact and effect.

1. ....

....

2. ....

....

3. ....

....

Need more practice?

Tackle the other writing task on page 71.

Remember to focus on careful selection and review of your vocabulary.

How confident do you feel about each of these **skills**? Colour 🖉 in the bars.

1 How do I explore vocabulary choices and their effects?

2 How do I use figurative language for effect?

3 How do I ensure my vocabulary creates the right effect?

Answers

Unit 1

Page 2

(1) For example: story not obvious, story is told in 'flashback', first person so readers empathise.

Page 4

(1) For example: first-person narration to create empathy for camel.

Unit 2

Page 10

(1) It is hard to see a definite point of view. The student feels the internet has both advantages and disadvantages.

Page 12

(2) Teenagers.

Unit 3

Page 18

(1) For example: flashback, truth withheld until end of story.

(2) For example: starting with climax or resolution.

(3) For example: narrator could stop and help Tom.

Page 19

(1) (b) For example: details in exposition could be discarded. For example: French ski instructor or best friend could be discarded.

Page 20

(1) The resolution is, perhaps, the weakest way to start as it instantly gives away the lie.

Page 21

(1) (a) Either description or conflict as neither reveal the lie.

(b) Enigma will perhaps be the most amusing as it refers to 'tall tales'.

Unit 4

Page 27

(1) (a) Point 4 is perhaps too obvious/weak.

(b) Points 3 and 5 could be linked to form a single, more developed point.

(2) Point 7, as most parents believe strongly in the value of revision.

Page 28

(1) 1 = A, 2 = B, 3 = D, 4 = C

Page 29

(1) Student A, as the controversial idea comes towards the end, making the conclusion more powerful.

Unit 5

Page 34

(1) Paragraph 2 uses repetition for effect with the word 'still' used to emphasise the aunt's formality and old-fashioned views.

(2) For example: synonyms could be used for 'mistake'.

(3) Overuse of stand-alone discourse markers means the paragraph loses fluency.

Page 35

(3) To put it simply, I feel there is too much emphasis on academic subjects. There is no longer any time in the curriculum for the arts, despite evidence that suggests artistic and creative subjects are essential for the development of personal expression. In my experience, students who take a balanced mix of academic and artistic subjects suffer less stress.

Page 36

(1) Expecially for <u>my aunt</u>.
<u>My aunt</u> is the only woman
One word from her can turn the air <u>at a family dinner</u> into ice; not even my father dares to cross her.
It was <u>at a family dinner</u> that the seed of my mistake was first sown ...

Page 37

(1) This student could have:

• replaced some of the repeated ideas and words with synonyms for 'test' and 'student' – for example, *assessment, young people, teenagers*

• used reference chains to refer to the same idea without repeating it – for example, *this means that they, it causes a problem because*

Page 38

(1)

For example:

I believe that we need to open up a debate about the purpose of education. We need to think about whether education is intended to impart knowledge, or whether its purpose is merely to prepare children for work. Significantly, education for its own sake would mean children spending more time studying the arts and being allowed to follow their interests rather than being forced down a rigid curriculum path.

Our current inflexible curriculum model has led to a lack of physical education in schools.

Unit 6

Page 42

1. A mood of suspense is created by the first two sentences, particularly as 'ordinary day' is emphasised by a short sentence.

3. a For example: 'I always want to win', or 'Life is a game for winners.'

Page 43

1. For example: 'I nearly didn't hear her.' Creates suspense as well as emphasises the narrator's surprise.

2. For example: 'I want to win.' Emphasises the word 'win'.

Page 44

1. For example: the second version as the short sentence at the end makes the writer's negativity about winning very clear.

Page 45

1. My wife hates my obsession with winning; nowadays I always play to lose.

   Society needs winners; we all love an underdog though.

   I told him I would die rather than admit my mistake; he just smiled.

2. Having being both a winner and a loser, I have come this conclusion: winning is fantastic, but losing means you don't need to try quite as hard!

Page 46

1. For example: Stop what you are doing. Just for one moment. Imagine a world that contains no element of competition, no arena where you can be number one, no stadium full of people who will cheer your progress or applaud your success. Everybody is equal. It sounds wonderful: no losers, no disappointment, no failure. You might long for such a society; I don't. It wouldn't, unfortunately, suit my intensely competitive nature. It doesn't matter whether I am playing a board game, taking a test at school or running the 100 metres. I always want to win.

Unit 7

Page 50

1. Annotations should note the withholding of important information in both extracts.

Page 51

1. a For example: I realised the time had come to make a stand when I saw it under my brother's bed. And: he was keeping a snake in his bedroom.

2. For example:
   The summer beach in our market square.

   1. Sandcastles, bright plastic buckets and spades, people struggling with the origami of deckchairs, hands sticky from candyfloss that melts in the mouth.

2. Children grizzle with boredom; parents sigh with exasperation: the summer holidays are here.

3. Men in shorts despite the chill in the air.

4. The great British seaside.

Page 52

1. For example: The snake hissed and began slithering my way.

2. a I clenched my fists, took a deep breath and started to edge silently towards the door, eyes never leaving the beast.

Page 53

1. For example: An excited crowd was at fever pitch as the bass guitarist (on time for once in his musical career) came on stage and began the sound check.

2. For example: Several years ago – although it still feels like yesterday – I decided to take a stand against my brother's vile and completely inexcusable behaviour.

3. For example: Beaches are the perfect setting for a romantic evening encounter – until the tide comes in.

Page 54

1. Annotations should cover sentence structures and lengths, punctuation and positioning of key information.

Unit 8

Page 58

1. For example: 'discomfiture' creates too formal a tone.

2. Paragraph has slightly hyperbolic, strident tone and lacks sophistication – for example: 'inconsiderate, lazy, foul-mouthed yobs' and 'innocent frail old ladies'.

Page 59

1. a For example: Contrary to the negative images painted by the press, in the majority of instances an examination of the way teenagers spend their time reveals that, on the whole, they live exemplary lives.

   b 'young people' has connotations of maturity, whereas 'teenagers' suggests irresponsibility.

2. For example: Regular readers of your newspaper might be interested to hear about Ellie Hughes who, despite frequent bouts of serious illness, spends much of her free time assisting at a local charity hospice for terminally ill children.

Page 60

1. a Sam finally had some hope that this would stop her being so weak and timid.
   Embarrassment would flood through me if laughter hit at the wrong moment.
   Knowledge of what was to come could have prevented my tears.

2. Nobody hears for instance, about John Edwards, whose lengthy, and blistering, charity walk raised thousands of pounds.

Page 61

(1) **a** For example: A brief glance at the tabloids on any given day reveals a plethora of tales condemning young people.

(3) **a** 1C, 2A, 3B

Page 62

(1) Annotations should cover register, abstract nouns and noun phrases and the use of ambitious vs simple vocabulary.

Unit 9

Page 66

(1) For example: 'armies of sunbathers' suggests they are literally attacking the beaches.

(2) For example: 'small kingdom of beach' is over-elaborate and a mixed metaphor in same sentence as 'armies'.

Page 67

(2) **a** Sentence A, as it takes a personal tone and emphasises that a chicken nugget starts life as an animal that is then cruelly treated.

(3) For example: A regular diet of fast food can condemn young people to a lifetime of poor health.

Page 68

(1) For example: 'daily fix' suggests fast food is a dangerous drug.

(2) For example: young people might appreciate it as it creates a humorous image.

(3) The second. Examples of figurative language should be explained.

Page 69

(1) For example: The majority of British parents care deeply about their children and it is therefore difficult to understand why they regularly serve them harmful substances that will damage their long-term health.

(2) For example: The wind sang in the trees ~~and the branches waved~~ beneath an inky black sky. Thin, ~~dingy~~ rain ~~spat and~~ drizzled. From under an umbrella of dripping leaves I could see it - just out of my reach, ~~a glistening jewel~~ teasing me from the shadows. ~~The bitter juice of~~ fear filled my mouth as I stretched out my hand to grasp my prize.

(3) It reads like a list of language techniques – e.g. rhetorical question, statistics, list, metaphor. It would be better to develop some of the points in more detail.

Page 70

(2) For example: 'Towers of slimy burgers and mountains of greasy fries' creates an unpleasant image and suggests fast food is always served in unnecessarily large portions.

(3) For example: 'tell' = persuade.